Flowers in Acrylic

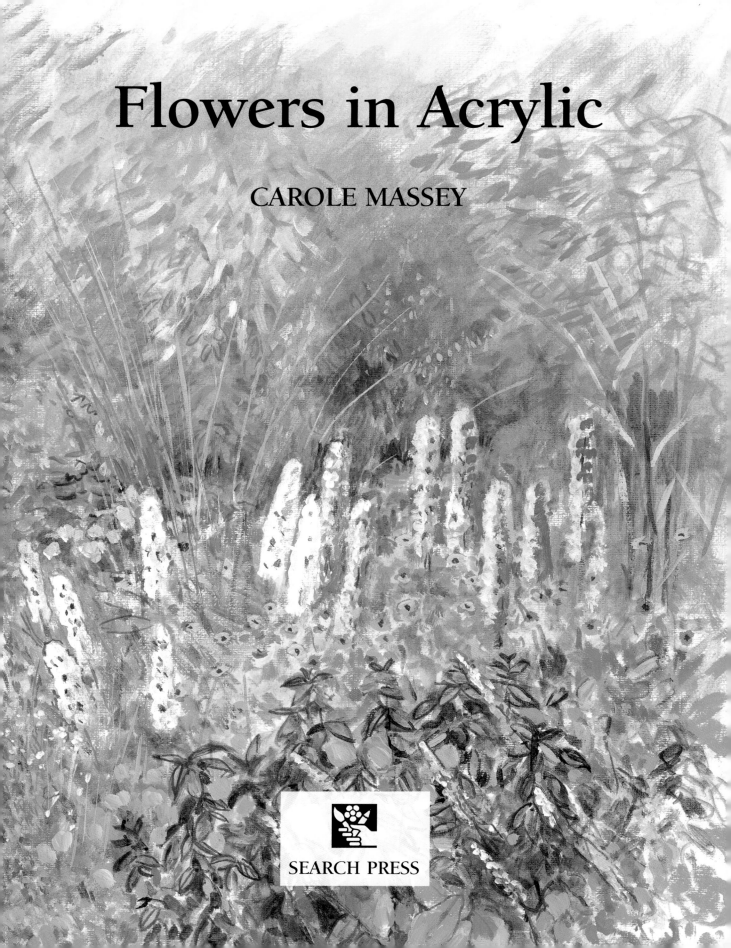

Flowers in Acrylic

CAROLE MASSEY

SEARCH PRESS

First published in Great Britain 2004

Search Press Limited
Wellwood, North Farm Road,
Tunbridge Wells, Kent TN2 3DR

Reprinted 2005

ISBN 0 85532 853 3

The publishers and author can accept no responsibility for any
consequences arising from the information, advice or instructions
given in this publication.

Suppliers
If you have difficulty in obtaining any of the materials and
equipment mentioned in this book, then please visit the Search
Press website for details of suppliers: www.searchpress.com

Alternatively, you can write to the publishers at the address above
for a current list of stockists, including firms who operate a mail-
order service, or you can write to Winsor & Newton requesting a
list of distributors.

Winsor & Newton, UK Marketing
Whitefriars Avenue, Harrow,
Middlesex, HA3 5RH

Publishers' note

All the step-by-step photographs in this book feature the
author, Carole Massey, demonstrating how to paint flowers
in acrylic. No models have been used.

Manufactured by Universal Graphics Pte Ltd, Singapore
Printed in Malaysia by Times Offset (M) Sdn Bhd

*Thanks to my gardening friends and family who have
provided inspirational subjects for this book: Bob Shuck,
Rhona Rosier, Sally Tollhurst, Bob Finch, Betty Pope,
Ann Bromfield and Eric Massey. My grateful thanks to
Ally, Roz and Juan at Search Press and to Eric and Charity
for their unfailing help and enthusiasm.*

Cover
Sweet Peas
47 x 37cm (18½ x 14½in)

*This is one of the most popular garden flowers, and is also a
favourite of mine.*

Page 1
Sunflowers
45.5 x 56cm (18 x 22in)

*These sunflowers stood in a vase but I rearranged them to
produce this stylised composition. I used thick layers of
cadmium yellow, cadmium orange and raw sienna for the
petals and burnt sienna and purple as well as burnt umber for
shading and emphasis. The complementary colour to yellow is
purple, so I made the background a bluish purple.*

Page 3
Rhona's Garden
46 x 30cm (18 x 12in)

*To paint this border in bright summer sunshine I used 'high
key' tones: light and bright, to build up the colour in thin
transparent layers after masking out the palest flowers.*

Opposite
Hollyhocks
15 x 39cm (6 x 15½in)

*The bluish shadows help delineate the frilly petals of this
quintessential cottage garden plant while the background
pattern of pure blue and green brush strokes makes the
subject leap off the page.*

Page 6–7
Daffodils in the Park
47 x 37cm (18½ x 14½in)

*The challenge when painting this scene was to create a sense
of distance and scale in an outdoor environment over which
one has little control. I returned to the same spot, at the same
time of day over a two week period, adding foreground detail
afterwards in the studio from photographs. Only the nearest
flowers need to be painted with any sort of accuracy.*

Contents

Introduction

Flowers are an ideal subject for the artist. In the garden, from the emergence of the first snowdrops, through the glorious profusion of summer blooms to the rich, vibrant colours of autumn, there is constant inspiration. Any time of year, a wonderful array of cut flowers and pot plants is available.

Before the seventeenth century, flower painting ranked low in comparison with traditional portraiture and landscapes. But as the Dutch trade in rare flowers from the Middle East grew, exotic bulbs became a valuable commodity, and the fashionable gentry commissioned paintings of their prized specimens as proof of their wealth and social status. Today, Van Gogh's *Sunflowers* is one of the world's favourite and most widely recognised paintings.

Acrylics are a really versatile painting medium. Fast-drying, odourless, flexible and non-yellowing, they can be used on almost any prepared surface. Gels or mediums can vary their consistency from matt to glossy, from thick to thin or add texture.

The styles used in this book range from watercolour-type techniques to thick palette knife painting, and I have used methods designed to help both the newcomer to acrylics and the more experienced user to deal with the inspiring subject of flower painting. I have shown how to paint a simple pot plant using transparent washes; a rose archway in a summer garden and an oriental lily using thick brushwork and a painting knife. I shall also look at flower shapes, colour mixes, composition, tonal contrast, foliage, as well as supports and materials.

I hope this book gives you the confidence to explore the infinite variety of techniques possible with acrylic paints and opens your eyes to the simple joys of flower painting, so you will enjoy my vision and feel confident to use this exciting medium. Happy painting!

Materials

An artist's materials are quite personal. Everyone has their favourite colours, brushes, and working methods. These are some of mine, but acrylics are really versatile and as your confidence grows you will adapt what you use, and how you use it, to your own requirements.

One of the delights of acrylics is their speed of drying. Take care never to let paint dry on your brushes or it will ruin them. I use two water pots: one for rinsing out brushes; the other with a drop of liquid soap added to stand dirty brushes in for cleaning later. Remember always to put your brush in water after using it.

Acrylics are water soluble when wet and permanent when dry. They produce little in the way of odour or fumes and are inflammable, flexible and non-yellowing. Acrylics should never be used with solvents, turpentine or oils, but different makes of paint can be mixed quite readily. It is best to use acrylic medium to thin the paint; if you do use water be sparing as thinning with too much water reduces the adhesion of the paint.

Supports

What you paint on is called a support. Acrylics are generally used on paper, canvas or canvas board, but they can be used on cloth, leather, metal, glass, china and even walls – in fact, almost any surface as long as it is properly prepared. Textured acrylic paper is a good surface to work on – see instructions for stretching paper on page 11. Prepared canvas can be made of linen, cotton or flax or a mixture of fibres. It is probably the best, but it is also the most expensive.

A range of different supports

Wet palette system

Because acrylics dry so quickly I always use a wet palette system. This is a lidded tray that is lined with a layer of absorbent paper, then a layer of translucent paper. I wet both layers, then put out my colours and mix my paints on the translucent paper surface. Spraying the tray occasionally with water prevents the surface drying out so your paints will stay workable for days or even weeks.

This is how my palette looks when I have been painting for a while. When the mixing area becomes too dirty, I replace the top layer and transfer any unused paint to this. I re-use the absorbent layer and dampen both layers again.

Brushes

I use both nylon and bristle brushes in all sizes and shapes: round, filbert, flat, long flat or rigger, depending on the application. I often keep a brush for each colour I am working with, standing each in water until I need it again. Different makes of acrylic brushes vary, so exact sizes are difficult to give, but the photograph shows a good basic range. Clean brushes with soap and water.

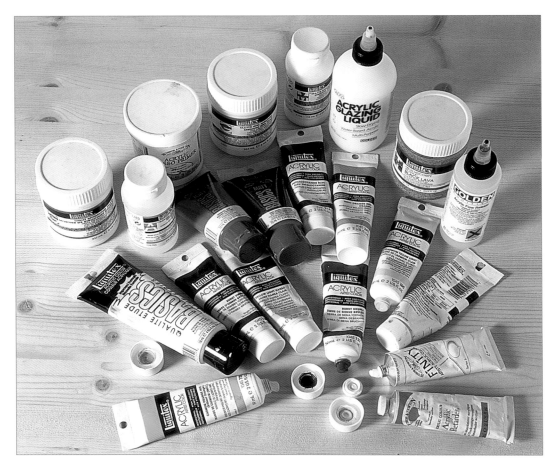

A range of paints, gels and mediums

Paints, gels and mediums

The characteristics of acrylics can be changed more readily than any other painting medium, so there are many exciting possibilities. They can be thickened or thinned without losing pigment strength, or made matt or glossy. Drying time can be slowed, or absorbency increased; textures can be created using gels containing things like sand, flakes, lava and beads. I have included some of the mediums I use, but there are many others you can try.

Paints are sold in tubes, bottles or even tubs for painting very large areas. Fluorescent, metallic and interference colours are also available.

Gloss medium and varnish is what I use in most of my paintings as a blending medium and to thin paint. For mixing paint, it is interchangeable with

blending medium, which may not be so readily available. It can also be used as a final varnish.

Retarder slows the drying time of the paint for fine detail work, and for easier blending.

Heavy gloss gel is a high-viscosity gel that can be added to the mixed paint to thicken it and retain brush or knife marks. It dries to a glossy shine.

Modelling paste can be mixed in to mould and sculpt the paint when wet. It can also be allowed to dry, then sanded and carved.

Flow enhancer

This improves the flow, absorbency and blending qualities. It can be used to thin paint for glazing.

Other equipment

Brown gum strip
This is used for stretching your work – see the instructions below.

Masking tape
Use this to fix paper to your drawing board.

Masking fluid
Use this to reserve fine details, or on areas that might otherwise be covered by a wash. Remove it when the painting is completely dry by rubbing lightly with your finger.

Wedges
These are used in the corners of prepared canvases to increase the tension.

Craft knife
Use this for sharpening pencils.

Pencils
I use B and 2B pencils for sketching.

Toothbrush
This is useful for producing splattering effects – see page 22.

Painting knife
Use a shaped painting knife for impasto work. A palette knife (not shown) is ideal for mixing large quantities of paint.

Eraser
I use a putty eraser which can be shaped and leaves no residue.

Stretching paper

Stretched paper always dries completely flat. You will need a sponge, a drawing board and four lengths of brown gum strip cut slightly longer than the sides of the paper. Wipe the wetted sponge over the drawing board, then place the paper on the board and wet that too. Stick down the gum strip, overlapping the paper by at least 6mm (¼ in). Allow to dry naturally. When the finished painting is completely dry, remove it by cutting between the paper and gum strip using a craft knife.

Colour	Tint
Hansa yellow light	
Cadmium medium	
Cadmium orange	
Napthol red light	
Cadmium red	
Quinacridone violet	
Dioxazine purple	
Phthalo blue	
Cobalt blue	
Ultramarine	
Raw sienna	
Burnt sienna	
Burnt umber	
Phthalo green	

Colours

Do not be impatient when mixing colours: it can take some time to achieve the right hue. Always try out the mixed colour before using it on your painting. If you think it might change, let it dry thoroughly to estimate colour shift.

The **primary colours** yellow, red and blue cannot be made from any other colours. **Secondary colours** are made by mixing two primaries: orange (yellow plus red); green (yellow plus blue) and purple (red plus blue). To reproduce the flamboyant, clear colours of nature, it is often best to use ready-mixed single pigment secondary colours like cadmium orange, dioxazine purple or phthalo green. They are far brighter than colours mixed using two primaries, and the effect will be much more vibrant – see page 46 *Orange on Blue*. **Complementary colours** are pairs of colours that sit opposite one another on a colour wheel and balance and enhance one another: blue and orange; red and green; yellow and purple. Blue can be enlivened by placing orange next to it. Be aware of the merit of complementary colours, particularly when mixing shadows: instead of using black or brown to darken, add the complementary colour to create more interesting effects. Mix a touch of purple into the shadow on a yellow daffodil petal, or naturalise an area suffused with green by adding a little red or brown.

Opacity and transparency

Information on whether colours are transparent (TP), translucent (TL) or opaque (O) will be given on the label of most good-quality paints. Transparent colours allow colour underneath to show through and are ideal for glazing. Translucent colours allow some light to pass through. Opaque colours reflect light, give the best coverage, and therefore make most impact. White is used to lighten colours or create tints: I buy large tubes as I use more of it than any other colour. Titanium white is bright, opaque, and ideal for highlights, while zinc or mixing white is softer, transparent and ideal for tints – see left.

Warm and cool colours

Knowing when to use warm or cool colours will produce more effective results. Cool lemon yellow plus a greenish blue such as phthalo blue will make a bright spring green, while cadmium yellow, which is warm, plus a reddish blue such as ultramarine will make warm olive green. A cool red such as quinacridone violet mixed with cobalt blue will make a beautiful purple, whereas a warm red such as cadmium red used with the same blue will produce a far greyer or browner result.

Colour shift

This effect occurs because the acrylic/water emulsion is milky when wet and may appear slightly lighter. As the water evaporates the binder becomes clear and the colour can darken slightly. The effect is less pronounced with modern acrylics.

Flower colours

This 'colour wheel' shows some of the most useful mixes.

Red (nasturtium)
cadmium red medium and cadmium orange

Orange (gazania)
cadmium orange and napthol red light; burnt umber and red markings

Bluish red (lavatera)
quinacridone violet and white

White (hellebore)
white with a touch of phthalo green plus quinacridone violet

Yellow (tulip)
cadmium yellow with a touch of cadmium red medium; a touch of purple in the shadows

Purple and lilac (polyanthus)
purple, ultramarine and white

Warm blue (cornflower)
cobalt and white

Green-blue (Himalayan poppy)
phthalo blue and white

Mixing greens

Practise mixing different greens to add depth and interest. In general, bluer cooler colours recede and warmer colours come forward in a painting. Hansa yellow or cadmium yellow light will produce a cooler, more acid green, whereas cadmium yellow medium will make a warmer olive green. A small amount of red or burnt sienna added to a bright green will neutralise it. Try mixing some of these examples to give you an idea of the wide variety of hues that can be achieved.

Phthalo green and hansa yellow

Permanent green light and ultramarine

Cobalt blue, cadmium yellow and white

Cadmium yellow and ultramarine

Phthalo green, lemon yellow, dioxazine purple and white

Permanent green and cadmium red

Cadmium yellow and phthalo green

Tip

Try to paint in this sequence: bright – dark – light. Paint the general colours and tones first, then the darkest areas. Put in the lightest colours and highlights last.

Canna Lily in Sunlight
20 x 36cm (8 x 14in)

It was a very hot day when I painted this, so I had to work rapidly as even with a retarder added to my paint, it was still drying fast. I captured the glowing orange, red and green striped foliage first and then added a patchwork of brush strokes using purple, phthalo green and burnt sienna to create a strong dark background in contrast.

15

Flower shapes & drawing

Though there is an emphasis on painting in this book, I cannot overestimate the importance of drawing. Accurate observation, sketching the plant growth, and understanding its shape and form, will greatly improve a finished painting. Always try to draw what you see, not what you *think* you see. As with any other form of drawing, be sure to look at the proportions, comparing the height to the width of the flower or plant, and observing the negative shapes – those spaces between the flowers and foliage or between one petal and the next – which will help you to draw the rest more precisely.

   Begin your study by sketching lightly with a B or 2B pencil. When you are happy with your drawing, go over it using a neutral colour that will blend in with the colours in the painting. I usually use raw sienna, burnt sienna or cobalt blue. As you redraw, do not merely outline your pencil drawing but keep observing the subject, altering and improving, making each stage exploratory.

Round

Simplify these chrysanthemum heads by thinking of them as a series of discs, turning towards and away from the viewer. The pattern and centre of these flowers form a series of concentric circles – which when viewed from an angle make up a series of ellipses. The flower head is not flat but dips in the centre, so observe carefully how the ellipses change in shape.

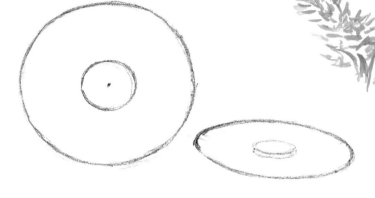

Trumpets

For a trumpet-shaped flower like these daffodils, lightly draw a circle or ellipse and in the centre, a cylinder, flared at the open end. Six equally spaced points on the circle mark where the tips of the petals touch it. Details like the frill at the trumpet mouth and the ribs in the petals can be added afterwards.

17

Multi-headed

In this example of a rhododendron, the overall shape is spherical but the flower head is made up of lots of smaller round flowers. Treat it as a group of individual round shapes, noting how the ellipses become shallower as they move over the sphere.

Bells

For each individual flower on this Canterbury bell, lightly draw an angled T shape and construct the bell shape round it, with two equal halves either side of the vertical line, and an ellipse across the bar of the T. Turning your drawing upside down can help you to construct equal halves.

Spikes

Flowers like these delphiniums are made up of a series of smaller flowers, positioned round a cylindrical shape that comes to a point at the top.

Stars

For a star-shaped flower such as this nicotiana, lightly draw four, five or six lines radiating from the centre of a circle or ellipse to points on the rim, to establish the centre of each petal.

Composition

Start by making a small, simple thumbnail sketch so you can see whether the layout and tones look right. Try to avoid a strong vertical or horizontal emphasis in the centre of your composition, placing it instead about a third of the way into the picture plane – the 'rule of thirds'. Where these lines divide are the focal points, which are the ideal places to place an accent – see the large tree in *Daffodils in the Park*, page 6–7 or the fountain in *Hollyhocks Against the Wall*, page 41. A repeated motif is often interesting – see pages 22 and 23. Group warm and cool colours to help balance the composition.

When you have worked out the composition, enlarge it to fit your paper or canvas. Look at the *negative* shapes – the spaces between the flowers – to aid accuracy. If you are painting outdoors, look at the light source. If you intend to work for any length of time, how quickly will the shadows change and alter your chosen scene? Sometimes it is best to paint for a limited period, at the same time, for several days running. You can set up two or three paintings this way.

Imperfect composition

* *The jug has been placed centrally.*

* *The shape of the white cloth seems to merge awkwardly with the jug's neck.*

* *In the background, a strong vertical hangs off the edge of the composition.*

* *The eye is led out of the picture by strong diagonals in the folds of cloth and the fruit at the painting's edges.*

Better composition

* *The slightly off-centre jug makes the composition more interesting.*

* *The simplified background enhances the composition.*

* *The fruit by the jug helps to ensure that the flowers are the focal point.*

* *The plainer background helps to emphasise the jug's shape.*

Tip

You may find a viewfinder useful to help to decide how much to include in a painting, and its format.

Opposite
Bouquet in Blue Jug
27 x 35cm (10½ x 14in)

I had always wanted to use this blue jug in a painting and the colours of a lovely bouquet I was given complemented it perfectly. I used a multi-coloured cloth to echo the blue, orange and yellow in the arrangement and began by dotting in the relative positions of the flower centres and drawing in the vase lightly. I had decided to alter the background to suit my composition – see the sketches opposite – but was not happy with my first choice of a neutral mix of raw and burnt sienna and white. I left it on my easel for several weeks waiting for inspiration, then a painter friend visited and suggested that I should try reds. Hey presto, it worked – thanks Sue!

Pink Geraniums in Niche

25 x 36cm (10 x 14in)

The wow factor! What made this a stunning subject for me was the pink of the geraniums leaping out of the dark recess. But there are other bonuses – the colour of the flowers is repeated in the container, and the shape of the container is echoed in the rectangular shape of the niche, outlined by the softer handling and colours of the surrounding wall. I used scumbling, dry brush and splattering effects to achieve the rough texture of the stonework.

Bob's Flags
51 x 38cm (20 x 15in)

*Three identical blooms, poised like ballet dancers
waiting to perform, set against a rich backdrop
of dark greens and blues. Although they look
unreal, this is just as I painted these flag irises in
a friend's garden. I used high key colours – pale
yellows, and delicate pale grey/blue shadows to
emphasise the brilliance of light filtering through
semi-transparent petals, which contrasted with
the cool pink, lilacs and bluish greens of a
mound of geraniums below.*

Tone

Tone means how light or dark something is. When I am asked to explain why a painting is not working, the most usual answer is lack of tonal contrast, which is more important than colour to make a painting come to life. Sketching a subject first in pencil can help to establish the tonal values before you start to paint. If you half-close your eyes before you look at your subject matter it will make it easier to assess the tones. Note that dark foliage can often be deceptively light in tone if it has a reflective surface.

Cactus With Pink Flower

35 x 52cm (14 x 20½ in)

I used grey textured paper and worked with matt acrylic paint enabling me to create a pastel-like effect in this staged still life. The reflected highlights and pools of fragmented sunlight through the leaves are in sharp contrast to the cast shadows and darker background tones.

Opposite
Hemerocalis and Ivy
28 x 38cm (11 x 15 in)

This hot, vibrant flower portrait is one in which sorting out the contrasting tones and colours was crucial to making this busy subject work. The alternating cool greens of the Hemerocalis leaves and the warm greens of the variegated ivy interweave across the painting surface.

Techniques

Acrylics can be used in many different ways, according to the effect you want to achieve. They can be used conventionally with a brush, or more thickly in an 'impasto' style with a painting knife. They can also be thinned and used like watercolour, though as each transparent layer dries it becomes permanent, and will not 'lift' or mix in and become muddied by successive layers. Their normal drying time is between five and fifteen minutes, but thick layers may take longer. Extremely thick layers may take several days, but are still much faster drying than oils. These examples show a range of the techniques I use.

Perspective
First Daffodils

The trumpeting daffodil heralds the warmer seasons to come, but capturing their distinctive shapes can be a challenge. Their vibrant yellow heads seem to twist and turn against the backdrop of dull, bare earth. I used complementary colours – purples and blues – for the shadows in the trumpets and petals to make them look three-dimensional. Mix purple in with the browns to achieve consistency throughout the painting.

Glazing
Single Roses and Buddleia

I added blending medium to extend the colour without affecting its intensity, and built up thin, transparent layers of paint to achieve a subtle glow. I painted successive layers of greens in the foliage, working from light to dark. To lighten a colour when glazing, add more water and medium: never use white, which is opaque.

Thin to thick
Orange Tiger Lily

I drew the lily and complex leaves, observing the negative spaces. I started painting thin washes of colour for the background, flowers and leaves, gradually increasing the thickness of the paint on the plant: ultramarine, hansa yellow and white for the leaves, and cadmium orange and cadmium yellow on the bright flowers, where the paint was thickest, to make them stand out.

Rapid sketches
White Lily

For this study on acrylic/oil paper I used a watercolour technique that is useful for producing quick outdoor studies of growing plants. A few patches of undiluted pigment in the background suggest a backdrop of blue flowers that could be developed further.

Christmas Cactus and Wooden Mannequin

I used only a 6mm (¼ in) flat bristle brush for this loose and swiftly painted subject on rough watercolour paper, to take advantage of some fleeting winter sunshine streaming on to the window sill.

27

Primulas

Simple studies of flowers can be amazingly effective, but you do not need to spend a lot of money on expensive blooms. These little plants cost just pennies, and when you have finished painting you can put them in the garden. I used the plant as a starting point for my drawing, but changed details like the position of individual flowers and leaves to improve the composition. The final touch was the suggestion of a plant pot, replacing the uninspiring shiny plastic of the original pot with a more aesthetically pleasing hint of terracotta.

This was a quick, spontaneous study. The paint was used like watercolour, allowing the white of the paper to shine through thin applications of colour. The colours were mixed with water with a few drops of flow enhancer added to encourage the paint to mix better.

You will need

140lb (300gsm) semi-rough (Not) watercolour paper 25 x 30cm (10 x 12in)

Flow enhancer

2B pencil

Putty eraser

Brushes: No. 1 and No. 4 round

Paints: cadmium yellow light; cadmium yellow medium; cadmium red; raw sienna; ultramarine; phthalo blue; dioxazine purple; titanium white

The small potted plant

1. Using a 2B pencil, establish the main outlines of the plant.

28

2. Using the No. 1 round brush and cadmium yellow light, put in the yellow markings in the flower centres, wetting the outer edges with water to encourage the colour to run slightly.

3. Using the same brush and purple with a little ultramarine, put in the edges of the flowers, dampening the paper with water towards the middle of the flower to lighten the colour.

4. Using a slightly thicker mix of the same colour, darken the edge of the petals, leaving a tiny space of white paper between the flowers and wetting round the yellow where necessary.

5. When you are satisfied with the way you have built up the purple tones, leave your work to dry.

6. Using the larger brush, paint a mix of ultramarine and cadmium yellow light into the leaves. Add a little more ultramarine and work over them wet in wet with this darker mix so the colours blend slightly.

7. Using the same brush and a phthalo blue and cadmium yellow light mix, put a light wash of colour on the lower leaves.

8. Switch back to the smaller brush and continue to paint the leaves using a range of tones and colours.

9. Paint in the veins on some of the leaves...

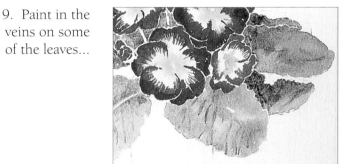

10. ... varying the amount of detail so that they do not all look the same.

11. Using the small round brush and a mix of ultramarine and cadmium yellow medium, put in the darker flower centres.

12. Using the small brush and raw sienna, add fine lines to the yellow markings in the centres.

13. Using the larger brush and a thin mix of cadmium yellow medium, cadmium red and a touch of purple, paint in the pot. While it is still wet, take some purple wash on the brush tip and touch it into the surface wet in wet to create shading.

The finished picture
I added the shadows under the pot using a thin mix of ultramarine and purple and re-established highlights using titanium white.

Five Pansies

Pansies are always delightful to paint, and are well suited to watercolour-type techniques. Each flower can be painted separately and – if necessary – on different occasions to produce a more formal composition. I used a wet in wet technique on HP watercolour paper and added a flow enhancer to encourage the paint to mix more freely. The darker markings in the centre of the petals were painted, then while they were still wet, they were encouraged to run by dampening the adjacent paper with a slightly wetted brush.

Vase of Roses

48 x 33cm (19 x 13in)

*This painting, in which I have used the acrylic paints just like
watercolour, demonstrates the versatility of the medium. The
advantage of acrylic over watercolour is that when they are dry, the
washes do not lift or mix and become dull. Some of the light areas,
especially in the vase, were achieved by reserving the white of the
watercolour paper, but in other areas, such as the tablecloth,
I added titanium white to emphasise the pattern.*

Rose Arch

Though drawing or painting from life is the ideal, it is not always possible. Photographs, particularly those you have taken yourself, are a good alternative. Do not try to copy them slavishly, as the photographic process can distort the true colours of nature: the sky may be bleached out, or shadows may appear unnaturally dark brown or black. Remember that you can move elements around to make a better composition – see page 20 – or simplify them, as I have done here. The dappled shadows across the path are very important: they increase the tonal contrast and really make the painting sparkle.

You will need

Canvas board 30.5 x 40.5cm (12 x 16in)

2B pencil

Putty eraser

Brushes: No 1, No. 4 and No. 8 round; No. 1 flat; No. 2 rigger

Paints: cadmium yellow light; cadmium yellow; cadmium red; quinacridone violet; cobalt blue; ultramarine; phthalo green; dioxazine purple; raw sienna; burnt sienna; titanium white

Gloss medium

The paint mixes I used:

Roses: quinacridone violet and white

Wall: cadmium yellow, raw sienna, burnt sienna and white

Path: cadmium yellow, raw sienna and white

Foliage: phthalo green and white; phthalo green and cadmium yellow light

Darker foliage: ultramarine and cadmium yellow

Very dark foliage: phthalo green and dioxazine purple

1. Using the 2B pencil, draw in the main outlines. Use grid lines to help position the main elements onto the canvas board.

2. Mix all the main washes and put in the first suggestion of colour as a placement guide.

3. Using the No. 8 brush, begin to block in all the main areas of colour.

4. Build up further tones, adding the mauve flowers and some darker detail to the tree in the top corner. Paint in the pot using cobalt blue.

5. Work on the foliage, adding touches of darker green leaves. Put in the shapes of the red flowers roughly using cadmium red. Paint in the plant, then add highlights to the pot using a mix of cobalt blue and titanium white.

6. Using the No. 4 brush and a mix of phthalo green and dioxazine purple, put in the dark green tones of the foliage round the roses.

7. Using the same deep green mix and brush, go into the lower right section of the painting and paint round the outlines of the leaves.

8. Using the same brush, lighten the roses with a mix of quinacridone violet and titanium white.

9. Using the No. 1 flat brush, add brickwork details to the wall using a mix of raw sienna and burnt sienna, adding some purple for the shaded side.

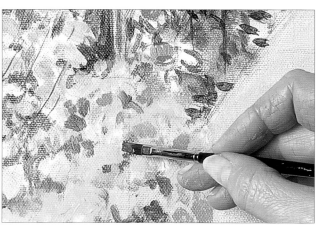

10. Mix white, cadmium yellow light and a touch of phthalo green and use the same brush to add the clump of light foliage at the front.

11. Add details of the second pair of arches with the dark green mix and the No. 2 rigger. Add spots of white for the flowers in the border.

12. Using a No. 4 brush and a mix of raw sienna and dioxazine purple, paint the dappled shadow across the path.

13. Using the same brush and shadow mix, paint in the lines of paving in perspective.

14. Using a mix of cadmium yellow light, raw sienna and titanium white, lighten areas of the path, going over some of the shadow if necessary. Using a mix of ultramarine and white, paint the delphiniums on the right.

Opposite

The finished painting

I applied a thin glaze of burnt sienna over the right hand area of wall and the path at the lower edge of the canvas to make the colour warmer, thus creating a greater sense of depth. Using the dioxazine purple and phthalo green mix, I added more shadow detail to the foreground foliage by picking out the negative spaces. Notice how the greatest amount of detail is reserved for the plants that are nearest. Finally I added any really bright highlights that were needed on the roses, the centres to the lilac poppies, the arch and the path to complete the painting.

*The photograph
I worked from*

Three Roses
27 x 38cm (10½ x 15in)

*All too often, I see something that would make a wonderful painting but
have no time to sit down and paint it. Photographs are the only option,
but often the subtlety of the colours is lost and the backgrounds become
dark and flat, so they need enhancing. I brought these wonderful, full-
blown roses back to life on white linen-finish acrylic paper, by enhancing
the pinks and yellows. I used warm blues and greys to make the
background interesting and to contrast with the flowers.*

Opposite
**Hollyhocks
Against the Wall**
24 x 37cm (9½ x 14½ in)

*The perspective of the wall,
paving slabs and hollyhocks
leads the eye to the focal
point of the painting, the
fountain. The tone of the
hollyhock stems and buds is
dependent on whether they
are set against a dark or a
light background.*

Stargazer Lilies

Stargazer lilies are a delightful subject. I took a single stem to study and stained the whole surface of the paper before starting to paint. To capture the vibrancy of the flowers, I blocked in the basic tones first, then built up the intense tones by adding layers of colour. I used blending medium with water to mix the colours, and added gels in the final stages of the painting to make the stamens and markings on the petals three dimensional. I used gloss gel as a blending medium rather than water to lighten the colours, as it keeps the colour transparent and allows the drawing to show through. The background behind the flowers was darkened to increase tonal contrast.

You will need

Textured acrylic paper 43 x 53cm (17 x 21in) stretched on a board

2B pencil

Brushes: range of rounds and filberts including a No. 8 bristle filbert and a No. 1 rigger – see note on brush sizes, page 9

Paints: cadmium yellow; raw sienna; quinacridone violet; burnt sienna; phthalo blue; cobalt blue; dioxazine purple; burnt umber; titanium white

Mediums: gloss medium; heavy gloss gel; thick gel

1. Using a 2B pencil, take time to make an accurate drawing.

2. Using the No. 8 filbert and a mix of raw sienna, burnt sienna and blending medium, stain the surface with a thin wash that allows the drawing to show through.

3. Using the Nos. 6 and 8 round brushes and a mix of cobalt blue and cadmium yellow, begin to block in the leaves and stems. Add a touch of phthalo blue to the mix for the darker tones.

4. Using the No. 8 brush and a mix of quinacridone violet and white, paint the pink flowers. Use a deeper mix of the same colours in the centre and paint the frilly edge white.

5. Using the staining mix with a touch more burnt sienna added, plus a little dioxazine purple, and a large brush, darken the background behind the flowers.

6. The buds contain hints of pale green and pale pink. Darken the leaves behind the flowers to make them stand out even more using the same mix as in step 3.

7. Using the Nos. 6 and 8 brushes, carry on adding more detail and depth to the flowers. Darken the pink with blue or purple for shading.

8. Mix heavy gloss gel with white and a No. 1 rigger, put in the edges of the petals.

9. Using the same brush and a mix of cobalt blue and cadmium yellow, start to work on the flower centre and the filaments of the stamen.

10. Using a mix of burnt sienna and purple, paint in the characteristic spots on the petals.

11. Using a large brush, glaze the background with a thin wash of burnt sienna, purple and blending medium. Let some of the brush marks show.

12. Using a mix of burnt umber and cadmium yellow with thick gel added, paint the brown anthers on the tips of the stamens. This will make them stand out from the surface of the painting.

Opposite
The finished picture

I added white highlights to the leaves and stamens and adjusted the background, darkening behind the light areas and lightening where necessary behind dark leaves and parts of the flowers.

Orange on Blue
37 x 28cm (14½ x 11in)

I love the vibrant contrast between the bright orange poppies and the vivid blue sky – see Complementary colours, page 12. I used masking fluid to conceal the poppy heads enabling me to paint the stalks and sky. I added the strong cadmium orange and yellow after removing the masking fluid.

Opposite
Red Poppies
30 x 43cm (12 x 17in)

These flowers have quite a crinkly surface, and when the sun shines through them, the bright red petals can look orange or crimson. I added modelling paste to the paint and used a painting knife to apply thick textured layers of red, orange and crimson with a mix of purple and phthalo green for the dark centres. I put in the background foliage of warm and cool greens quite roughly using a mixture of criss-cross brush strokes and the painting knife.

Index